LIMITS
OF THE
VISIBLE

REPRESENTING
THE GREAT
HUNGER

Cork City Library
WITHDRAWN
FROM STOCK

D1610325

LUKE GIBBONS

CORK CITY
LIBRARIES

CONTENTS

Figure 1 | Micheal Farrell. *Black 47*

Vision is the art of seeing things invisible.

Jonathan Swift (202)

REPRESENTING THE GREAT HUNGER

Writing in 1989 on the approach of many Irish historians to catastrophe in the past, Brendan Bradshaw noted a tendency "to avert one's gaze from the sufferings of past generations or to seek to immunize them by recourse to the distancing devices of academic discourse." While such attempts to "remove the pain from Irish history" became an orthodoxy, the "bitter reality, recalled in song and story, continues to haunt the popular memory" (Bradshaw 341).[1] But if the tendency was "to avert one's gaze," the question arises whether *images* could also bear witness to the "catastrophic dimension" in Irish history. As in the "distancing devices" of historians, detachment and disinterestedness are also invoked as the basis of visual representation—"the role of the audience is to see, not to respond" (Sennett 209)[2] but a powerful countercurrent in aesthetics turns on the "theatricality" of the image, its potential to address and indeed *implicate* the spectator in the field of vision. In these circumstances, exhibition space and cultural context—of both production and reception—become central to aesthetic experience, encouraging participation and engagement on the part of the viewer rather than a dispassionate gaze.[3]

This is seen to telling effect in one of the major exhibits of Ireland's Great Hunger Museum at Quinnipiac University, Micheal Farrell's *Black '47* (1997–98) [Figure 1], in which the dramatic shaft of light that bisects the painting appears to emanate from outside the picture, from a window on the adjoining museum wall, breaking the boundaries between pictorial and gallery space [Figure 2]. It is as if the spectator is drawn into the scene depicted on canvas. The picture plays on what is inside and outside the frame, as in the glimpse of feet beneath (or behind) a grim display of exhumed skeletons, which suggests a painting within a painting (but which also recalls the discarded shoes of Nazi death camps). Charles Trevelyan, the architect of British policy during the Famine, stands in the dock, as a hound, one of the symbols of Ireland in nationalist iconography, looks askance while fleeing from the scene of the crime. Trevelyan points to the potato as the cause of disaster; the crowd in the

Figure 3 | Pádraic Reaney, *Departure* [detail]

darkened gallery points to the victims, not as authors of their own fate, but as the key exhibits or witnesses for the prosecution. The bisecting shaft of light all but bleaches color out of those caught in its beam, including members of the British establishment who turn their back on the proceedings, and whose white outlines mimic the skeletons opposite them in the lower half of the canvas. Though one of the sources of cultural collapse during the famine was the breakdown of sympathetic ties among Irish people—self-preservation often being achieved at the expense of loved ones—two of the skeletons are shown with arms wrapped in solidarity around one another (thus giving the lie to Andrew Marvell's "The grave's a fine and private place, / But none, I think, do there embrace" ("To his Coy Mistress" 31–32)).[4] In an earlier preparatory work of Farrell's in the museum, the skeleton is interred beneath the courtroom, and such isolation is also the fate of the buried bodies in Pádraic Reaney's *Departure* [Figure 3], in which emigrants depart for a future seemingly unaware of the dead beneath their feet: " ... a footstep / That leaves an imprint on the air," as Paddy Bushe writes in "Toponomist," his elegy on a famine landscape (qtd. in Crowley, Smyth, and Murphy 586).

Walking to invoke the memory of the dead is also part of Rowan Gillespie's sculptures, *Statistic I* and *Statistic II* [Figure 4], in which a roll call of victims' names is engraved on the "ground" under bereft figures. The spare architecture and unadorned walls of Ireland's Great Hunger Museum itself resemble a workhouse but also, in a more elliptical way, the inner distribution of space resembles a ship—the steerage on the enclosed ground floor, and the more open deck upstairs, accessed by a narrow stairwell with wave-rippled handrails. It is in this sense that both the logic of display and the works themselves cultivate a sympathetic engagement with the harrowing experiences of the Great Famine and its aftermath. But these aesthetic strategies have also to contend with one of the indictments of the image as an ethical resource, namely, that its sensual or personal appeal is limited to the exercise of sympathy or compassion, and it is not capable of addressing wider issues of justice, duty or obligation. Sympathy, on this moral compass, points to voluntary and discretionary responses to suffering, which are all the more commendable for being beyond the call of duty. The difficulty

Figure 4 | Rowan Gillespie. *Statistic I* and *Statistic II*

with this is that it runs the risk of recapitulating the terms of state policy during the Great Famine, in which the alleviation of distress and suffering was left to charity and philanthropy—the domain of sympathy rather than justice—the latter constituting a duty of care incumbent on the government itself.

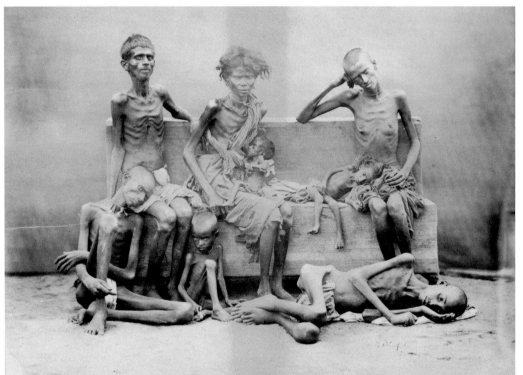

Figure 5 | Willoughby Wallace Hooper. *Madras Famine Victims*

It was considerations such as these that led Susan Sontag to note, in her famous critique of the photographic image, that "while it can goad conscience, it can, finally, never be either ethical or political knowledge. The knowledge gained through photographs will always be some kind of sentimentalism, whether cynical or humanist" (Sontag 24). In a similar spirit, W. B. Yeats remarked that it is difficult to make poetry out of passivity, on the grounds that even if images of helpless suffering arouse feelings of pity, they still take from the dignity of the victim (Yeats xxxiv). Pity, as Hannah Arendt argued, brings with it a paternalism that converts passivity into dependency, and transforms suffering into scenes of subjection (Arendt 85). This can be seen in one of the earliest photographs to document famine, a disturbing picture taken by Captain Willoughby Wallace Hooper of Madras famine victims in 1876 [Figure 5]. As Luke Dodd notes, the skeletal figures are posed indoors as if for a family photograph, but one is so weak as to require support from a barely visible rope off-stage: "These images compromise the dignity of the subjects, and do little more than offer them up as fetish-like objects for a Western audience" (qtd. in Crowley, Smyth, and Murphy 667).

THE DARK SIDE OF THE LANDSCAPE

Representations of famine are rare in nineteenth-century photography. Though the first decade of the new medium coincided with the Great Famine in Ireland, no photographs were taken, as many commentators have noted, of the unfolding disaster. There are many reasons for this, perhaps the most obvious being the cumbersome and expensive nature of the technology in its early days. There were also ideological reasons: enterprising landlords such as Lord Clonbrock and Edward and Louisa King-Tenison were among the pioneers of Irish photography but they could hardly have been expected to show up the iniquities of the system that kept the Big House in its privileged place. Photographs do survive from this early period, but they are mainly portraits of public figures (including convicted Young Ireland political leaders, perhaps the earliest photographs taken in prison), landscapes, street scenes, antiquities, and, in rare cases, of rural laborers.[5] That very few of these early photographs attend to the dark side of the landscape may be due to the fact that "the philosophical and ethical concept of documentary" had not "entered the cultural lexicon of photography among the Anglo-Irish" (Carville 66). Yet this is not to say that there was no awareness of the *image as evidence*, or of the capacity of graphic realism to furnish pictorial proof of what could be conveyed only indirectly through writing. It is the shortcomings or, more accurately, *encodings* of this evidence that are of interest here, for they suggest that, in addition to technology and political ideology, pictorial *genres* and representational *codes* were also responsible for obscuring, or screening off, the "terrible realities," in Charles Gavan Duffy's phrase (qtd. in Crowley, Smyth, and Murphy 485). The shift from Romantic Ireland and the picturesque undoubtedly added a greater documentary value, but there were also, as critics such as Sontag suggest, certain ethical limits to the visible itself as it attempted to hold the mirror up to the desolation of the Irish countryside, "to add the last touch of horrible grotesqueness to the picture" (qtd. in Crowley, Smyth, and Murphy 485).[6]

The first systematic attempt to visually depict the Great Famine was undertaken by the Cork born artist, James Mahony, working on behalf of *The Illustrated London News* **[Figure 6]**. Mahony was chosen to report both verbally and visually on the famine-ravaged districts of west Cork, most notably Skibbereen. The editorial thinking behind the decision to send a visual artist highlights some of the discrepancies between word and image in representations of the Famine:

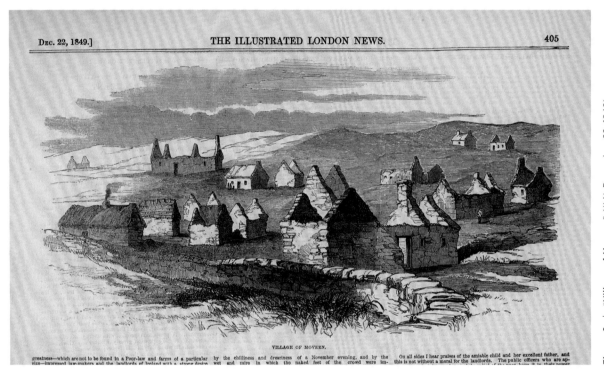

Figure 6 | "Village of Moveen" (*ILN*, December 22, 1849)

The accounts from the Irish provincial papers continue to detail the unmitigated sufferings of the starving peasantry … With the policy of ascertaining the accuracy of the frightful statements received from the West, and of placing them in unexaggerated fidelity before our readers, a few days since, we commissioned our Artist, Mr. James Mahoney [sic], of Cork, to visit a seat of extreme suffering, viz., Skibbereen and its vicinity, and we now submit to our readers the graphic results of his journey ("Sketches in the West of Ireland," Feburary 13, 1847, qtd. in Mark-Fitzgerald 189).

The image is meant to bear witness and to authenticate verbal accounts; in fact, it held back from depicting the worst atrocities. There are some grim pictures—including searing images of children digging for potatoes, and of Bridget O'Donnel (unusual in its naming of an individual)—but there is no depiction of the hideous scenes described in print that haunted future generations: people eating grass with green-stained mouths, dogs digging up cadavers, bodies buried like refuse in mass graves.

Though the bodies of the suffering are pathetic and clearly in distress, they are far from the emaciated skeletons familiar in present-day photographs of contemporary famines. It is as if words could go into places where images feared to tread. Explaining this visual restraint in depicting the true horror of the Famine, Emily Mark-Fitzgerald suggests that had images been too explicit, they may have repelled viewers rather than elicit the required sympathy: "The intention of these articles [and images] to function as motivators of charitable action further limits the possible modes of representation: too graphic an image, and the viewer moves quickly past pity or sympathy through to disgust" (195). It is in this context that the anomalies of the image become evident, for the implication here is that even if photography were technically advanced as a medium in the 1840s, there would still be a relational "ethics of representation," a need to take account of the spectator in rendering the point of view of the victim. It is this two-way process in the dynamics of vision that is of central importance, for it implies that so far from negating experience, a certain reticence or refusal "to show all" is required if an image is to elicit an ethical rather than a sensational (or even sentimental) response, in the end.

In this context, it is striking that Edmund Burke, in an attempt to convey the horrors of an earlier Bengal famine to the British House of Commons, employed a "judicious obscurity" to close the gap between sentiment and justice. Condemning the depredations of the East India Company under Warren Hastings that plunged the Carnatic region into "the jaws of famine," Burke remonstrated that "All was done by charity that private charity could do," but "it was a people in beggary; it was a nation which stretched out its hands for food":

Every day seventy at least laid their bodies in the streets, or on the glacis of Tanjore, and expired of famine in the granary of India. I was going to awake your justice *towards this unhappy part of our fellow-citizens, by bringing before you some of the circumstances of this plague of hunger. Of all the calamities which beset and waylay the life of man,* this comes nearest to our heart ... *but I find myself unable to manage it with decorum; these details are of a species of horror so nauseous and disgusting; they are so humiliating to human nature itself; that, on better thoughts, I find it more advisable to throw a pall over this hideous object, and to leave it to your general conceptions* (*Works,* iii 160–61; my emphasis).

Burke was not contesting the need for precision, statistics and accurate information, indeed he excelled in such a grasp of detail in his extensive reports on India. Rather he was raising the question of whether such a cold eye is sufficient to prompt people thousands of miles away to do something about it. It is striking that though he drew on compassion ("this comes nearest to our heart"), he also appealed to *justice,* stipulating that the proper response to famine lies not only in the domain of charity but also of duty and obligation—or as he termed it elsewhere, "the obligations written on the heart" (*Works,* iv 214). This fusion of sentiment and justice may indeed be best served by bringing aesthetics to bear on ethics, infusing moral principles with the lived experience of suffering. It is true that by putting a human face on suffering, and appealing to the senses, images give the lie to more abstract, statistical accounts of famine, but does it follow that representations can only tug at heartstrings, moving viewers to tears but seldom to indictments of injustice? Sentimental images may certainly prompt charitable and philanthropic responses but are they in a position to raise questions about *the system* itself, to point to injustices stemming from the impersonal forces of an unfettered market, or laissez-faire policies prohibiting state intervention, even in conditions of crisis and emergency? An impersonal response is in keeping with this objectification of human beings, and it is precisely for this reason that the image has recourse to the aesthetics of "theatricality" described above, in its determination to accost a detached or averted gaze.

BOY AND GIRL AT CAHERA.

Figure 7 | "Boy and Girl at Cahera" (*ILN*, February 20, 1847)

BRIDGET O'DONNEL AND CHILDREN.

Figure 8 | "Bridget O'Donnel and Children" (*ILN*, December 22, 1849)

THE UNFLINCHING EYE

One of the most notable aspects of the images exhibited in Ireland's Great Hunger Museum is the *direct address* of starving figures to the viewer. This "unflinching eye" (O'Sullivan, "Lines of Sorrow" 10) is evident in James Mahony's illustrations "Woman Begging at Clonakilty" and "Boy and Girl at Cahera" **[Figure 7]** (particularly the accusing stare of the boy), in the famous 1849 illustration "Bridget O'Donnel and Children" **[Figure 8]**, and in later paintings such as Lilian Lucy Davidson's *Gorta* **[Figure 9]** (previously referred to as *Burying the Child*), in which the central male figure looks up from his digging to make direct eye contact with the viewer. At times this look can be supplicating or even winsome, as in Daniel MacDonald's *Irish Peasant Children* (1847), but even then supplication does not rule out making a demand on the spectator. In William Carleton's novel *The Black Prophet* (1847), written during the Great Famine but set during the earlier famines of 1817 and 1822, a starving mother with dying children importunes the viewer/reader:

Her eyeballs protruded even to sharpness, and as she gazed around her with a half-conscious and half-instinctive look, there seemed a fierce demand in her eyes that would have been painful were it not that it was occasionally tamed down into something more mournful and imploring by a recollection of the helpless beings that were about her (346).[7]

Here melancholy tames the demand on the spectator but elsewhere, pathos and even prostration are bound up with calls for *justice*, and a determination to resist oppression. In Richard D'Alton Williams's poem, "Lord of Hosts," published in John Mitchel's *United Irishman* in 1848, the appeal to heaven is not linked to quietism but to insurrection:

Figure 9 | Lilian Lucy Davidson, *Gorta*

Lord of Hosts! In vain for pity
Tyrants long we prayed, but now
To thee we cry from plain and city
Rise, and judge between us, Thou!

If we seek but justice purely
Earth and Hell our foes may be;
Thou wilt bless our banners surely,
And Thy smile is victory ...

Lord of Hosts! In tears before Thee
See the prostrate people kneel—
Hear the starving poor implore Thee—
Smile on Freedom's sacred steel!
(qtd. in Morash, *The Hungry Voice* 239)

In Alanna O'Kelly's video installation, *No Colouring Can Deepen the Darkness of Truth* (1992) **[Figure 10]**, a display of supplicating hands caked in clay is linked visually to the telltale signs of famine lazy beds in fields, the furrows and ridges of the landscape simulating the shape of fingers and outstretched palms. The reduction of a human being to begging is linked to the social injustice embedded in land and soil, the political source of the collapse of an entire cultural ecosystem.

In her critique of the politics of pity, Hannah Arendt took issue with public expressions of sympathy and compassion on the grounds that they lack the *universal* remit of justice. Prefiguring the terms of Sontag's indictment of the image, Arendt

Figure 10 | Alanna O'Kelly, *No Colouring Can Deepen the Darkness of Truth*

contends that the introduction of feeling or passion into politics, as in mercy and compassion, or the desire to square civic culture with the impulses of the heart, carries with it the risk of converting politics into mere personal sentiments. This is a fundamental category-mistake, for while compassion assumes a face-to-face encounter, and can only be directed at individuals, justice is best served by anonymity and a dispassionate exercise of reason:

Compassion, by its very nature, cannot be touched off by the sufferings of a whole class or a people, or, least of all, mankind as a whole. It cannot reach out farther than what can be suffered by one person and still remain what it is supposed to be, co-suffering. Its strength hinges on the strength of the passion itself, which, in contrast to reason, can comprehend only the particular, but has no notion of the general and no capacity for generalization (85).

Is it the case, however, that "the strength of the passion" induced by, or brought to bear on, a particular situation is strictly limited to those circumstances, and cannot extend beyond the individual case? Writing of the social collapse of 1847, Canon John O'Rourke wrote that the sense of calamity lay "not in new forms of suffering amongst the famine stricken people" but precisely "in its universality"—that is, a systemic failure on the part of the state and the economy. The problem then becomes one of representing universal or abstract systems, the "dismal science" of economics, without inducing the forensic approach that allows people to stand idly by: "The starving poor suffered so intensely and in such a variety of ways, that it becomes a hard task either to narrate or to listen to the hideous story. To say the people were dying by the thousand of sheer starvation is too general to move our feelings" (qtd. in Morash, Writing the Irish Famine 150). The problem then may not be that of extrapolating from the particular to the universal but the opposite one of putting flesh on statistics, of preventing the treatment of people as objects or dispensable commodities to facilitate the expansion of free trade. As Luc Boltanski writes, it is difficult to describe "the bodies of dead children during a famine, with the same kind of precision and detachment one would use to speak of a system of economic regulation, a policy of regionalism, or a plan for a road network" (43)—though one discourse was reduced to the other in Government policy during the Great Famine.

This clash of registers informs a real-life incident recounted in the Rev. Sidney Godolphin Osborne's *Gleanings in the West of Ireland* (1850), in which the author, traveling with a companion, describes a journey from Leenane to Westport on the Western coast. A young girl, about twelve years of age, began to run doggedly alongside the carriage without directly asking for anything, and try as they would, the travelers could not dissuade her. Osborne remarks on his irritation at the manner in which "her silent wearying importunity" challenged not only their privacy but also the principles of political economy: "I read fresh lectures on the evil of being led from sound principles, by appeals to our pity, through the exhibition of what excited our wonder," but his friend relented in the end, and gave the young girl fourpence.

"I confess I forgave him—it was hard earned, though by a bad sort of industry"
(91–92). The inability of political economy to do justice to the condition of the Irish
poor is noted once again in a review in *The Illustrated London News* (February 26, 1853)
(qtd. in Cullen 88) of Robert George Kelly's large-scale canvas, *An Ejectment in Ireland*
(1848–51, private collection) **[Figure 11]**, exhibited in London in 1853:

*R. G. Kelly paints the horrors of "An Ejectment in Ireland" in a manner to move the
sympathies of the sternest political economist, if not to gratify the sense of the critical
observer. Ruthless policemen swaggering over kneeling and imploring females; whilst
old men and infants are scattered helplessly in the melée.*

Figure 11 | Robert George Kelly, *An Ejectment in Ireland (A Tear and a Prayer for Erin)*

Yet, on account of the politically charged subject matter, the painting is
found offensive: "In a word, the subject is vulgarly treated, and artistically,
is of very inferior merit."

The image of victims reduced to soliciting pity rather than justice is only possible because the right to subsistence, and the most basic right to life, had been expelled by the harsh economic logic of free trade and the sovereign rights of property. The English MP George Poulet Scrope condemned the restriction of human welfare to bare contractual relations, devoid of any customary laws or duties, an outcome not of the invisible hand of the market but of "the meticulous elimination of all non-market behaviour that is considered aberrant or undesirable" (Nally 7–8). Though Edmund Burke is excoriated for his claim that "the laws of commerce are … the laws of God," it is often overlooked that he also proclaimed an equally immutable right to subsistence:

The benefits of Heaven to any community ought never to be connected with political arrangements, or made to depend on the personal conduct of princes, in which the mistake, or error, or neglect, or distress, or passion of a moment, on either side, may bring famine on millions, and ruin an innocent nation perhaps for ages. The means of the subsistence of mankind should be as immutable as the laws of Nature, let power and dominion take what course they may. — Observe what has been done with regard to this important concern (*Works*, iii 181; my emphasis).

That the right to life, or subsistence, took precedence over privileged property rights was a constant refrain in criticisms of government policy leveled by figures as diverse as James Fintan Lalor or Archbishop John Hughes of New York, but their calls for justice fell on deaf ears. According to Archbishop Hughes, under the British Treasury:

The sacredness of the rights of property must be maintained at all sacrifices, unless we would have society to dissolve itself into its original elements; still the rights of life are dearer and higher than those of property; and in a general famine like the present, there is no law of Heaven, nor of nature, that forbids a starving man to seize on bread wherever he can find it, even though it should be the loaves of proposition on the altar of God's temple. But, I would say to those who maintain the sacred and inviolable rights of property, if they would have the claim respected, to be careful also and scrupulous in recognizing the rights of humanity (Hughes 22).

Rather than casting the right to life aside, Hughes continued, governance has a duty to protect the well being of society: "Society, that great civil corporation which we call the State, is bound so long as it has thy power to do so, to guard the lives of its members against being sacrificed by famine from within, as much against their being slaughtered by the enemy from without" (22). For James Fintan Lalor, writing in a more trenchant vein to the *Irish Felon* in 1848, there is "no right of property which takes away the food of millions and gives them a famine—which denies to the peasant the right of a home, and concedes, in exchange, the rights of a workhouse" (qtd. in Fogarty 65). As David Nally wryly notes (168), the inversion of values under market economics was such to "be labeled a 'criminal' actually meant recapturing certain rights that were otherwise denied to subaltern groups—after all, even the petty criminal could claim a right to ample sustenance independent of any 'test of destitution'" (that is, unlike applicants for poor relief).[8]

The identification of the market as the arbiter of justice, as in the economic thought of Adam Smith, removed everything outside market logic from the domain of rights and obligations, thus relegating welfare and redress of poverty to philanthropy (well meaning and even necessary as it was).[9] In Ireland, the poor were excluded not only from the benefits of "the invisible hand" of commerce but also from the ministration of charity, due to the abrogation of even a semblance of sympathetic ties between Britain and Ireland. When the last soup kitchen closed in October 1847, Lord Clarendon wrote in despair to the Prime Minister, Lord John Russell: "*Ireland cannot be left to her own resources,* they are manifestly insufficient, we are not to let the people die of starvation." The reply was stark and to the point: "The state of Ireland for the next few months must be one of great suffering. Unhappily, the agitation for Repeal has contrived to destroy nearly all sympathy in this country" (qtd. in Woodham-Smith 317; emphasis in original). It was this absence of "sympathy," or the imagined community of a common culture, which set the seal on Ireland's precarious position within the United Kingdom. Though some historians have contended that the treatment of the Irish peasantry was no different than that meted out to the English working class, contemporaries such as Lord Clarendon, the Lord Lieutenant, had little doubt that the true analogy of the Irish rural poor was not the British urban proletariat but the aboriginal first peoples of Australia: "I would sweep Connacht clean and turn upon it new men and English money just as one would to Australia or any freshly discovered colony" (qtd. in Moran 84).[10] Isaac Butt pointed out that the Famine exposed an irrevocable rift between colonial power and the colonized, and that the process of ostracizing Ireland as a separate jurisdiction made a mockery of the Act of Union:

If the Union be not a mockery, there exists no such thing as an English treasury ... How are these expectations to be realized ... if, bearing our share of all imperial burdens — when calamity strikes upon us we are to be told that we then recover our separate existence as a nation, just so far as to disentitle us to the state assistance which any portion of a nation visited with such a calamity has a right to expect from the governing power? If Cornwall had been visited with the same scenes that have desolated Cork, would similar arguments have been used? (Butt 514: my emphasis)

Ireland's "separate existence as a nation" is borne out in a private note from Queen Victoria to Lord Russell in 1847, included in the collection of Ireland's Great Hunger Museum, in which she expresses her concern for Ireland: "The Foreign Affairs give the Queen great anxiety" **[Figure 12]**.

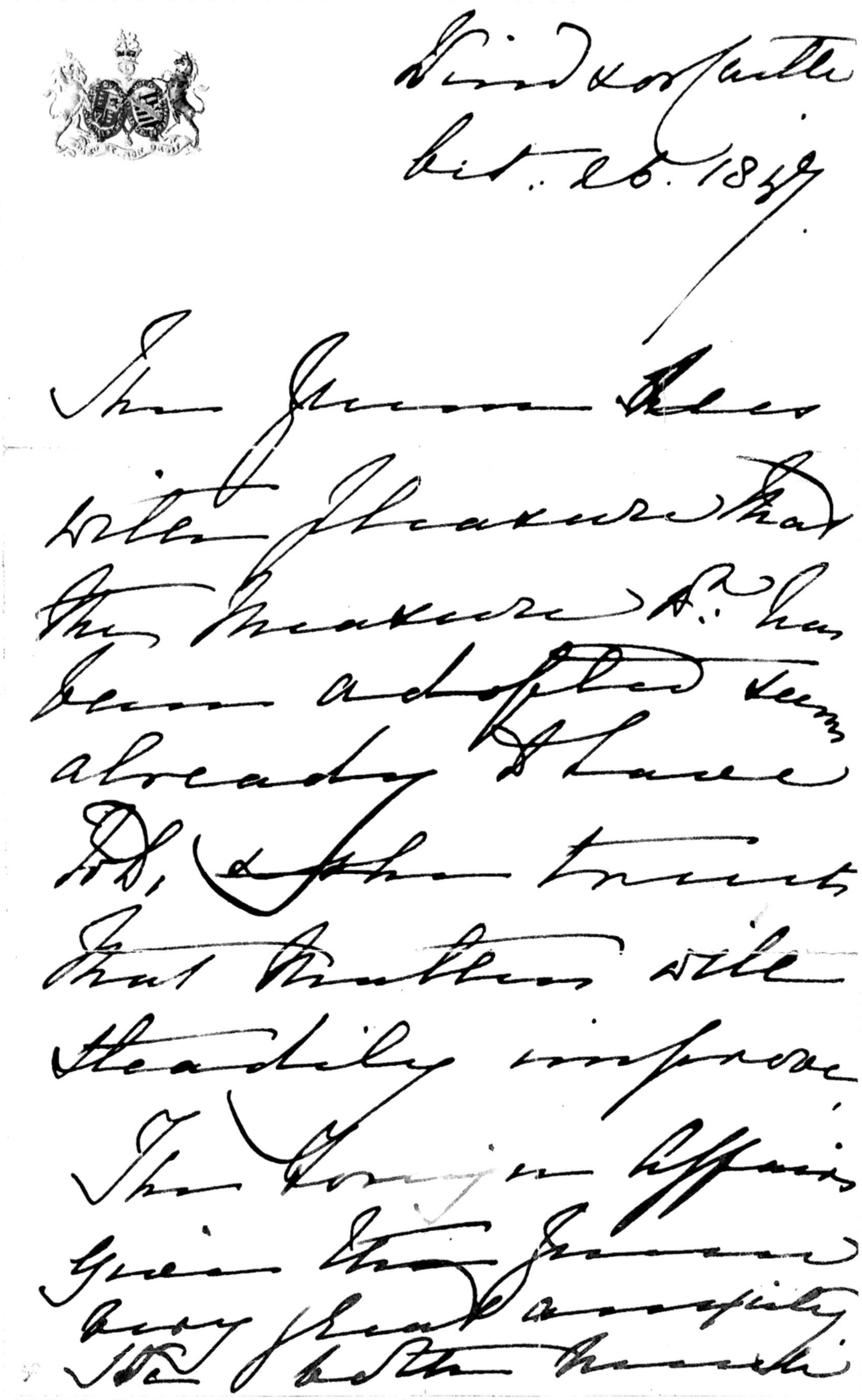
Windsor Castle
Oct. 26. 1847.

The Queen sees
with pleasure that
the measures &c. have
been adopted & seem
already to have
done good, & she trusts
that matters will
steadily improve.
The Foreign Affairs
give the Queen
very great anxiety

Figure 12 | Queen Victoria Letter [detail]

THE POLITICS OF VISION

In the photo-etchings of Geraldine O'Reilly's *Deserted Village, Achill Island* (2012) in Ireland's Great Hunger Museum, light is defined by the shadows thrown on the landscape since the nineteenth century. Grass-stubbled roads cannot find their way home. Abandoned gable walls loom like headstones and, from a distance, headstones themselves in graveyards seem to have more in common with the rocks around them **[Figure 13]**. It is not just absentee landlords but the populace itself that has gone missing. Writing about the same Mayo countryside one hundred years after the Famine, Ernie O'Malley noted that the land does not have to await representation but carries its own bereft expression: "Memory must play its part ... in enclosures of light-filigreed stone walls which map land hunger, or in unobtrusive cottages, dwarfed by mountain and hill to an almost tragic insignificance" (66). It is as if the surface is already etched, and photographs are not so much after the event as emanations from the same act of engraving. Though no one is watching, there is a sense that the fields are looking back, in the words of John F. Deane's antiphonal lines to O'Reilly's images: "[T]he way an urchin might once have watched / From a doorway."

The reciprocity of looking back raises a key ethical aspect of representations of atrocity, that is, the *obligation to look* rather to avert the gaze. This acquired a particular urgency in the twentieth century when faced with representing human beings at the limits of suffering, as in the Nazi death camps of World War II. Georges Didi-Huberman has noted that of the one-and-a-half million photographs of Nazi concentration camps, only four show extermination at work—badly exposed and distant images taken from a concealed camera at Auschwitz-Birkenau. The Nazis sought to hide the scene of extermination, though of course they could not conceal its effects. It is worth asking whether the failure to visually represent, or at least to publicize, their own lethal handiwork was due to a political failure of nerve, or perhaps as suggested above, certain limitations of the image itself. The four photographs of the death-camps were taken clandestinely at great risk by a number

Figure 13 | Geraldine O'Reilly, *The Deserted Village* [1 of 8 panels]

of "Sonderkommandos," the wretched prisoners selected by the Nazis to line up victims for the gas chambers, and to dispose of the bodies in crematoria afterwards. The purpose of the photos was to smuggle out proof of genocide in the camps to the Polish Resistance movement, the image indeed acting as evidence of the atrocities that were taking place: as late as October 1945, George Orwell could ask in print: "Is it true about the gas ovens in Poland?" (421)[11] As such, the photos were clearly meant to help in the liberation of the suffering inmates, but that is not how some critics received them when Didi-Huberman included the "images snatched from hell" (Didi-Huberman 3) in a controversial exhibition, "Memory of the Camps," in Paris in 2001. Bearing in mind Edmund Burke's admonitions against showing all in cases of extreme suffering, Didi-Huberman was taken to task for showing anything at all, for attempting to represent the unrepresentable.

Didi-Huberman was subjected to a series of bitter attacks from what he terms the "unimaginable" (19) school, a group that subscribes to the view that the Holocaust is in principle beyond representation. This included Gerard Wajcman, Elizabeth Pagnoux and—more ambiguously—Claude Lanzmann, director of the nine-and-one-half-hour documentary, *Shoah* (1985), which refused to show a single archival image of the camps. These critics argued that instead of furthering the cause of the prisoners, the images colluded in their humiliation and degradation, since to represent in such circumstances is to *affirm* what is represented: "no image can show absence," wrote Wacjman, "the image is always affirmable" (qtd. in Didi-Huberman 74). Yet, in the case of the Sonderkommandos, it can hardly be the case that they endorsed the scenes presented to the camera: they were engaged in the task of bringing what was hidden, or couched in euphemisms, to a public that had an *obligation* to know what was done in its name. "In Hitler's Germany," Primo Levi wrote, "a particular code was widespread: those who knew did not talk; those who did not know did not ask questions; those who did ask questions received no answers" (381).[12]

It is in this sense that faced with atrocity, the image, no less than the word, implicates the viewer, demands a response. The act of *staring*, as in so many Great Famine images, is emblematic here for, as Rosemarie Garland-Thomson asserts, the "address" of staring initiates an encounter among strangers: "This intense visual engagement creates a circuit of communication and meaning-making. Staring bespeaks involvement and being stared at demands a response …. Staring's brief bond can also be intimate, generating a sense of obligation between persons" (4–5). But if staring solicits the eye, the terror of empty sockets, the vacant stare into the void, are even more characteristic of Great Famine accounts and pictures. This commands a returned gaze with greater urgency, if only to ensure the spectator does not constitute the void on the other side—"the ghastly faces, hollow and shrunken, which I have seen, with death looking out of their eyes" (qtd. in McLean 116).[13] The obligation to look arises precisely on account of what is *not there*, absent from vision: the instinct to avert the gaze is in inverse proportion to the necessity of giving the dehumanized face full attention. "A black hole," writes Gilles Deleuze, "is what captures you and does not let you go. How do you get out of a black hole?" (Deleuze and Parnet 171). The trope of entering a dark, infested cabin with barely visible cadaverous figures—"black and bare / And doleful as the cavern of despair"[14]—became a standard trope of Famine travel narratives, and Ireland presented itself as a black hole to the dyspeptic eye of the Victorian writer and polemicist, Thomas Carlyle, as he ventured through the Irish countryside: "The history of [Ireland] does not form itself into a picture, but remains only a huge blot—an indiscriminate blackness, which the human memory cannot charge itself with … " (qtd. in Rigney 177). In Dorothy Cross's work *Endarken* **[Figure 14]**, an exhibit in her show "LANDscape" (2008) at the Dublin City Gallery The Hugh Lane exhibition "The Golden Bough," an image of a dilapidated thatched cottage is initially shown, its neglected surroundings overgrown with weeds and rushes. Both home and homeplace have reverted to emptiness and to accentuate the void, a black dot gradually enlarges from the center of the image to block/black out the screen. It is as if the "Iris" effect is the ineluctable mote in the eye confronting the post-Famine landscape, the limits of the visible excoriated by Thomas Carlyle.

Figure 14 | Dorothy Cross, *Endarken*

The picture that refuses representation at key moments, though realistic in form, is on a continuum with the obliquity required by the aesthetics of atrocity. The formal reticence that does not show all, leaving room for active responses that spectators *bring to* the image, is the grounds of the obligation to look. These are images, according to Didi-Huberman, "that we are inclined to refuse but that do not ignore us and, rather, beg for our gaze ... whose authors so ardently wanted us to pay attention to them" (74). Though the image may hold back, as we have noted, from depicting harrowing scenes of the kind that lend themselves to verbal description, the paradox is that when words fail, images step into the breach and come back to haunt us—whether in dreams, flashbacks, or indeed visual representations.

As the Land Question shifted from the state violence of the Great Famine in the 1840s to the agrarian violence of the Land War in the 1880s, new tensions between word and image began to appear in periodicals such as *The Illustrated London News*. Shrill denunciations of agrarian protest in the written text were counterpointed by vivid illustrations by artists such as Aloysius O'Kelly, that left the door open for opposing nationalist interpretations—the image, as it were, representing the return of the repressed in language (O'Sullivan, *Aloysius O'Kelly* 70). The inherent ambivalence of the image acts as a reminder that no matter how graphic or detailed the picture, there is still an excess of "the real" that eludes the frame. "Not all of the real is solvable in the visible," wrote Gerard Wacjman in his criticism of the exhibition of photographs from the death camps (qtd. in Didi-Huberman 59), without acknowledging that this is also Didi-Huberman's position in relation to the "lacunary image" (65). No image of atrocity can do justice to all there is to be known, but images can still induce a shock of recognition in the face of realities that others would prefer not to be shown. Walter Benjamin famously quoted Brecht to the effect that "Less than ever does the mere reflection of reality reveal anything about reality.

A photograph of the Krupp works or the AEG tells us next to nothing about these institutions" (213). Devoid of captions or a linguistic frame, images are unanchored, as Roland Barthes remarked (37–51), and can transmit even contradictory readings at one and the same time.

The role of the diverse written commentaries in *The Illustrated London News* was perhaps to anchor the image, but images can also be acted upon by other images: as John Berger suggests, a picture of a starving family in Bangladesh records a situation but tells us nothing about poverty or injustice, until it is juxtaposed with a picture of plenty in the West (171–72). Indirection can also open up the image, shifting attention away from the particular to forces beyond the frame or the field of vision. This is evident in the Francis Bacon-type imagery of Brian Maguire's *The World is Full of Murder* (1985) **[Figure 15]**, in which body parts are splayed in the foreground against a flame-like spurt of blood in the background. Anthony Trollope notoriously claimed that though the Great Famine was stalked by death, there was no pain: "There were no signs of acute agony, none of the horrid symptoms of gnawing hunger by which one generally supposes that famine is accompanied. The look is one of apathy, desolation, and death" (684–85). Maguire looks to visceral color and explosive gestures to visualize the pain, which also allows a generality that refers to other scenes of suffering (he mentions the mass starvation in Eastern Europe after World War II, and, closer to home, the murderous conflict in Northern Ireland). Abstraction in this sense goes beyond but does not deny the immediate, placing it in a wider comparative frame: as Maguire states, "The collective memory of 1847 enables us to hold this gaze on contemporary famine" (*IGHM Inaugural Catalogue* 28).

Figure 15 | Brian Maguire, *The World is Full of Murder*

Figure 16 | "The Famine Queen" (*L'Irlande Libre*, 1900)

The question of sympathetic relations concerns not only spectatorship in the gallery but also the wider question of the colonial observer's responses to the Great Famine, as noted at the outset in relation to Micheal Farrell's *Black '47*. A French cartoon of 1900, "The Famine Queen" [Figure 16], shows Queen Victoria attempting to shield her gaze from graveyard skulls (akin to the Farrell painting) and the smoking ruins of British rule in Ireland, thus incurring the obloquy of the refusal to look. Another cartoon in *United Ireland* in 1890 [Figure 17], shows a young woman wrestling with the specter of famine at her cottage door, while the Prime Minister Balfour turns his back on the scene to play golf on the manicured lawns in the background, his bent body and splayed legs mimicking the posture of the ghost.[15] To say that the scene of suffering *commands* a sympathetic reaction is not to say it is automatically induced: on the contrary, no image speaks for itself, and a myriad of responses is possible to even the most transparent rendering of reality. But not all responses carry the same

CORK CITY LIBRARIES

moral weight: that Nazis took photographs of round-ups and atrocities at death camps and failed to be moved by images which horrified viewers after the war, is on a continuum with the thinking that brought about the camps in the first place. It is for this reason that meaning is essentially *relational*, bound up with what is brought to an image as well as what is brought away from it. In the case of a failure to respond to acute suffering, "the form of concern which appears to the spectator," writes Luc Boltanski, "is can he avoid the register of 'shame,' 'bad conscience' or 'guilt' that shows up a clear moral inadequacy" (188). It is as if the refusal to respond to images of suffering in these circumstances is, in effect, to join the perpetrators of the injuries. Though much is made of "survivor guilt" and self-abnegation among the Irish peasantry, there is little evidence of personal shame or guilt among decision-makers over the Victorian holocausts that resulted from government policies: "These were highly conscientious men," wrote A. J. P. Taylor laconically, "and their consciences never reproached them" (153).[16] Presented decades later with a dramatic large-scale painting by Elizabeth Thompson (Lady Butler), *Eviction*, exhibited at the Royal Academy in 1890, Lord Salisbury, the Prime Minister, expressed admiration for the "breezy cheerfulness and beauty [of] the landscape" but had no sympathy for the subjects abandoned to the elements: "It makes me long to take part in an eviction myself whether in an active or passive sense" (qtd. in Cullen 114).

"Supplement Gratis with" "UNITED IRELAND." Saturday, August 23rd, 1890.

IRELAND WRESTLES WITH FAMINE,
WHILE
MR. BALFOUR PLAYS GOLF.

Figure 17 | "Ireland Wrestles with Famine while Mr. Balfour Plays Golf" (*United Ireland*, August 23, 1890)

PROJECTING THE NATION

Yet hubris was apparent at a "macro" rather than a "micro" level, in the contradiction which the occurrence of famine on its own doorstep presented to British claims to represent the highest point of human civilization. Notwithstanding Britain's self-image as the workshop of the world, officially celebrated in the staging of the Crystal Palace Industrial Exhibition in 1851, all was not well on the western front. A Manchester industrialist, Spencer T. Hall, was shocked on a visit to Ireland in 1849 to discover a mass grave outside Limerick "into which nearly two thousand bodies had been gathered in less than a month ... instead of being in some far off primitive land, I was in reality within twenty hours ride of home and among citizens of the same nation" (qtd. in Morash, *Writing the Irish Famine* 16). The shock here is not just at the level of suffering but that the "primitive" should co-exist within the home ground of the metropolis. Faith in progress was preserved in these circumstances relegating Ireland to the condition of a throwback, a "survival" of indigenous culture whose days were numbered precisely because of the Great Famine. As W. Nassau Senior, one of the architects of laissez-faire orthodoxy, expressed it:

In Ireland the consequence was famine ... a calamity which cannot befall a civilized nation; for a civilized nation ... never confines itself to a single sort of food, and is therefore insured from the great scarcity by the variety of its sources of supply. When such a calamity does befall an uncivilized community, things take their course; it produces great misery, great mortality, and in a year or two the wound is closed, and scarcely a scar remains (Nally 1).

Others had little doubt that the primitivism of Ireland was a result of progress, a product of imperial modernity. As if picking up on Nassau Senior's "scar" metaphor, Archbishop John Hughes of New York protested that while "there is no external wound, there is no symptom of internal disease," it was the invisible rather than the visible that inflicted the greatest damage. Though the state purported to guard the individual:

Figure 18 | Margaret Allen, *Bad News in Troubled Times*

against all outward violence; it merely encircled him around in order to keep up what is termed the regular current of trade, and then political economy, with an invisible hand, applied the air-pump to the narrow limits within which he was confined, and exhausted the atmosphere of his physical life (Hughes 22).

These subtle modes of extermination did not require blueprints or the battlefield, but this was only because in earlier periods, the groundwork had been prepared. Turning progress against itself, Hughes noted that during the Elizabethan conquest, famine was deliberately used to such an extent that beside it, "the Indian's tomahawk becomes a symbol of humanity" (19). It is for this reason that images of famine are haunted by absence as much as presence, and an aesthetics of disappearance acts as the visual counterpart of the Great Silence. While agency and policy were responsible for decision-making, the real moral culpability lay in the abandonment of justice to an abstract capitalist logic that worked its way implacably through the Irish countryside. But the invisible hand left very tangible effects, aided by an insensate colonial apparatus that gave the lie to any pretense of political legitimacy.

If we look again at Micheal Farrell's *Black '47* from this angle, it is possible to view it, literally, in a new light, as a visual world confined to sentiments (in Susan Sontag's terms) attempts to widen its remit to seek the redress of justice. Part of its impact turns on the improbability of the proceedings, for there was no likelihood of Sir Charles Trevelyan appearing in the dock: unlike the Nuremberg trials, there was no conspiracy behind the Great Famine, no round table conference at which it was decided to eliminate the Irish. There was nothing to hide: hence the white light which conveys the impression of full and frank disclosure. This is in keeping with the metaphor of light that informs the "Enlightenment," according to which, truth is the guarantor of freedom, and institutions such as the media play a key role in maintaining democracy. However, in a society of the spectacle, it may be the surfeit of information itself that is the problem: as Thomas Keenan notes, "all too often, there is more than enough light, and yet its subjects exhibit themselves shamelessly, brazenly, and openly" (438). What was done by the British Treasury during the Famine was done in good faith, adhering to a value system which prided itself on delivering democracy and freedom—and yet tens of millions died (if we add the other Victorian holocausts enumerated by Mike Davis).[17] This suggests, in Jean Baudrillard's terms, that "it is transparency itself that is the Evil," providing the alibi for the violence perpetrated in the name of progress (36). As Baudrillard also argues, it is precisely what is not shown that underlies the visible; hence in Farrell's painting, it is the Irish themselves who are in the dark, pointing to the destruction and suffering which had to be exhumed from oblivion.

Faced with the invisibility of the forces which brought about the crime, it is not surprising that the disaster was attributed to unseen agencies: to Divine retribution—a grim subaltern echo of the providentialism espoused by leading ideologues in the British Treasury—or else to terrifying visitations of the Otherworld, closer to Gothic fiction (Póirtéir 219–31).[18] One of the notable aspects of domestic interiors of Irish cottages in nineteenth-century painting is the unobtrusive appearance of popular prints on the walls in the background, and it is striking that the supernatural is a pervasive theme. These range from providentialist motifs, such as the self-immolation of the Sacred Heart picture in Aloysius O'Kelly's, *Mass in a Connemara Cabin* (1882), to devotion to the Madonna, juxtaposed against dreams of commodity culture in James Brenan's *The Finishing Touch* (1876) exhibited in Ireland's Great Hunger Museum. In another exhibit, Margaret Allen's *Bad News in Troubles Times* (1886) **[Figure 18]**, a grieving mother receives bad news, perhaps that her son has become a victim of the Land War, but over her shoulder a print shows landlordism as a bird of prey attacking Ireland personified as a woman, reversing the *Punch* cartoon of a year previously, "The Irish Vampire," which portrayed the vampire bat of Parnell and the Land League swooping on a sleeping maiden body.

That images of death and dispossession derived from the Great Famine became effective weapons in the Land War and the national struggle is evident from their spectacular use in later popular demonstrations and street propaganda. On June 22, 1897, the eve of Queen Victoria's jubilee, Maud Gonne (who christened Victoria the "Famine Queen") and James Connolly used a magic lantern to project images of recent eviction scenes to recall the famine dead, on a large screen in Rutland (now Parnell) Square, Dublin (Cullen 97–124).[19] Earlier, Connolly had organized a demonstration and mock funeral, attended by a crowd of ten thousand (including W. B. Yeats and John O'Leary), in which a coffin symbolizing the British Empire was thrown over O'Connell Bridge. To enhance the visibility of Maud Gonne's show, Connolly organized workers in Dublin Corporation to cut electric wires to black out competing elaborate city center electric displays in shop windows and streets celebrating the jubilee. The insulted authorities sent the police to attack the crowd, and an old woman was killed in the process. Maud Gonne recounts in her autobiography that she went to the aid of the woman:

Someone said: "This is your work, Miss Gonne. I hope you are satisfied." The girl kneeling beside the old woman said: "Mother wanted to see the pictures so I brought her when the crowd had gone and they have killed her." An ambulance arrived and lifted the dead woman and her daughter followed. A Man whispered to me: "We will avenge her, Miss Gonne," and rushed off with a group of men walking rapidly into the crowd (Gonne MacBride 218).

As a prelude to the 1798 Centenary commemoration the following year and subsequent anti–Boer War demonstrations, the spectacle of larger-than-life images of rural destitution using modern media technology proved a turning point in the political revival following the death of Parnell: "The outcome of the anti-Jubilee demonstration," according to Priscilla Metscher, "was to open the eyes of the general public to the fact that Dublin as a centre of loyalty to the British Empire was a myth that once and for all had been destroyed" (37). Though no photographs of the Great Famine have survived, photographs and other images of its legacy helped to ensure that the political administration responsible for the calamity would not survive itself in the twentieth century.

ENDNOTES

[1] Recent research on the Great Famine by historians and social scientists such as Cormac Ó Gráda, Christine Kinealy, Peter Gray, James S. Donnelly and, more recently, David Lloyd, David Nally, John Kelly, Enda Delaney and Ciarán Ó Murchadha, has done much to challenge the morally distanced approach criticized by Bradshaw.

[2] Sennett is writing of the "visual turn" towards design and spectacle in theatrical forms such as Richard Wagner's operas.

[3] In *Absorption and Theatricality: Painter and Beholder in the Age of Diderot* (1980), Michael Fried defends aesthetic "absorption" against the "theatricality" of the image that addresses a space outside the painting, beginning with the beholder but extending to the space of the museum and its social milieu. See Michael Fried (1980). For the range of strategies exploring "theatricality," see also Clare Bishop (2006).

[4] An Irish Folklore Commission respondent from Sneem, Co. Kerry, recalled that a farmer uncovered the bones of an old man and child while laying a fence near a house where a family had died from starvation, reporting that "the arm of the old man was around the child" (McLean 113).

[5] See Sean Sexton (1994), Sean Sexton and Christine Kinealy (2002), Edward Chandler (2001), Edward Chandler and Peter Walsh (1989).

[6] Gavan Duffy iterates the standard warning that "no words in a newspaper or elsewhere" can capture the horror before the eye; yet he only makes sense of what he sees in terms of literary and mythological analogies: "more debased than the Yahoos of Swift," "more frightful than the harpies." (Crowley, Smyth, and Murphy 485).

[7] For the gendered basis of this and related descriptions, see Margaret Kelleher (1997).

[8] Cormac Ó Gráda (10) notes that this might have been partially responsible for the dramatic rise in crime and the acute overcrowding of prisons during the Famine.

[9] In terms of economic orthodoxy, philanthropy or charity was also unwelcome as it encouraged Irish laziness or a "bad sort of industry," as Osborne described it (91–92). According to Charles Trevelyan, too much was done for the starving poor, and as a result they "have grown worse instead of better, and we must now try what independent exertion, and the operation of natural causes, can do" (Woodham-Smith 302). As against this, for the Society of Friends, philanthropy was necessary rather than discretionary (in keeping with Edmund Burke's view that faced with famine, charity was a "perfect" rather than an "imperfect" obligation (see Gibbons 2003).

[10] It is noteworthy that Clarendon makes no secret of the fact that Ireland is a colony, rather than an integral part of the United Kingdom.

[11] Orwell's essay was written in May 1945. Even after war ended, Orwell noted that "many English people have heard almost nothing about the extermination of German and Polish Jews during the present war. Their own antisemitism [sic] has caused this vast crime to bounce off their consciousness" (vol. 3 420–21).

[12] Heinrich Himmler on the annihilation of the Jews: "in public we will never speak of it … It was the tact which I am glad to say was a matter of course that made us never discuss among ourselves, never talk about it. Each of us shuddered, and yet each one knew that he would do it again if it were ordered, and if it were necessary" (qtd. in Dawidowicz 132).

[13] On arrival in Strokestown, Co. Roscommon, Somerville further noted: "The people are going about, those that can go about, with hollow cheeks and glazed eyes, as if they had risen from their coffins to stare at one another" (116).

[14] William Allingham, *Laurence Bloomfield in Ireland: A Modern Poem.* London: Macmillan, 1864 (qtd. in Cullen 111).

[15] These images are reproduced in (Gray, *The Irish Famine* 178) and (Crowley, Smyth, and Murphy 577).

[16] As Cormac Ó Gráda adds: "The fear that kindness would entail a Malthusian lesson not learnt also conditioned both the nature and extent of intervention ... Compassion on the part of the British elite was in short supply" (15).

[17] Davis, Mike. *Late Victorian Holocausts*. London: Verso, 2000.

[18] See also Gray (1999) and Morash (1996).

[19] See also Kevin Rockett and Emer Rockett (70–71).

WORKS CITED

Allingham, William. *Laurence Bloomfield in Ireland: A Modern Poem*. London: Macmillan, 1864. Print.

Arendt, Hannah. "The Social Question." *On Revolution*. Harmondsworth: Penguin, 1974. Print.

Barthes, Roland, "Rhetoric of the Image." *Image Music Text*, Trans Stephen Heath. London: Flamingo, 1984.

Baudrillard, Jean. "The Transparency of Evil." *Passwords*. Trans. Chris Turner. London: Verso, 2003. Print.

---. *The Transparency of Evil: Essays on Extreme Phenomena*. Trans. James Benedict. London: Verso, 1993. Print.

Benjamin, Walter. "A Short History of Photography." *One-Way Street*. Trans. Edmund Jephcott and Kingsley Shorter. London: New Left Books, 1980. Print.

Berger, John. *Ways of Seeing*. London: Penguin, 1972. Print.

Bishop, Clare. *Participation: Documents of Contemporary Art*. Cambridge, MA: MIT Press, 2006. Print.

Boltanski, Luc. *Distant Suffering: Morality, Media and Politics*. Trans. Graham Burchell. Cambridge: Cambridge University Press, 1999. Print.

Bradshaw, Brendan. "Nationalism and Historical Scholarship in Modern Ireland." *Irish Historical Studies*, xxvi, 104 (November 1989): 329–51. Print.

Burke, Edmund. "Speech on the Nabob of Arcot's Debts." *Works*, iii. 1785. London: George Bell, 1901. Print.

---. "Letters on a Regicide Peace (I)." *Works*, iv. 1796. London: George Bell, 1901. Print.

Butt, Isaac. "The Famine in the Land." *Dublin University Magazine* 29 (Apr. 1847). Print.

Bushe, Paddy. "*An Logainmneoir*/Toponomist." *To Ring in Silence: New and Selected Poems*. Dublin: Dedalus, 2008. Print.

Carleton, William. *The Black Prophet: A Tale of Irish Famine*. 1847. Shannon: Irish University Press, 1972. Print.

Carlyle, Thomas, ed. *Oliver Cromwell's Letters and Speeches*. Vol. 2. London: Chapman and Hall, 1857. Print.

Carville, Justin. *Photography and Ireland*. London: Reaktion, 2011. Print.

Chandler, Edward. *Photography in Ireland: The Nineteenth Century*. Dublin: Edmund Burke, 2001. Print.

Chandler, Edward, and Peter Walsh. *Through the Brass Lidded Eye: Photography in Ireland, 1839–1900*.

Dublin: The Guinness Museum, 1989. Print.

Crowley, John, William J. Smyth, and Michael Murphy, eds. *Atlas of the Great Irish Famine.* Cork: Cork University Press, 2012. Print.

Cullen, Fintan. *Ireland on Show: Art, Union, and Nationhood.* Farnham, Surrey: Ashgate, 2012. Print.

Dawidowicz, Lucy S. *A Holocaust Reader.* West Orange, NJ: Behrman House, 1976. Print.

Deleuze, Gilles and Claire Parnet. *Dialogues II.* Trans. H. Tomlinson and B. Habberjam. New York: Columbia University Press, 1987. Print.

Didi-Huberman, Georges. *Images in Spite of All: Four Photographs from Auschwitz.* Chicago: University of Chicago Press, 2012. Print.

Dodd, Luke. "Images of Famine: Whose Hunger?" *Atlas of the Great Irish Famine* Crowley, Smyth, and Murphy, eds. Cork: Cork University Press, 2012. Print

Duffy, Charles Gavan. "The New Nation." *The Nation*, 1 September 1849, reprinted in *Atlas of the Great Irish Famine.* Crowley, Smith, and Murphy, eds. Cork: Cork University Press, 2012. Print.

Fogarty, Lillian. *James Fintan Lalor: Patriot & Political Essayist (1807–1849).* Dublin: Talbot Press, 1921. Print.

Fried, Michael. *Absorption and Theatricality: Painter and Beholder in the Age of Diderot.*
Berkeley, CA: University of California Press, 1980. Print.

Garland Thomson, Rosemarie. *Staring: How We Look.* Oxford: Oxford University Press, 2009. Print.

Gibbons, Luke. "Did Edmund Burke Cause the Great Famine? Commerce, Culture and Colonialism." *Edmund Burke and Ireland: Aesthetics, Politics and the Colonial Sublime.* Cambridge: Cambridge University Press, 2003. Print.

Gonne MacBride, Maud. *A Servant of the Queen: Reminiscences.* 1938. Gerrards Cross: Colin Smythe, 1994. Print.

Gray, Peter. *Famine, Land and Politics: British Government and Irish Society 1843–50.* Dublin: Irish Academic Press, 1999. Print.

---. *The Irish Famine.* London: Thames and Hudson, 1995. Print.

Hughes, (Archbishop) John. *A Lecture on the Antecedent Causes of the Irish Famine in 1847.* New York: Edward Dunigan, 1847. Print.

Ireland's Great Hunger Museum Inaugural Catalogue. Hamden, CT: Quinnipiac University, 2012. Print.

Keenan, Thomas. "Mobilizing Shame." *South Atlantic Quarterly* 103: 2/3, Spring/Summer 2004: 435–49. Print.

Kelleher, Margaret. *The Feminization of Famine: Expressions of the Inexpressible?* Cork: Cork University Press, 1997. Print.

Levi, Primo. *The Reawakening.* New York: Simon Schuster, 1965. Print.

Mark-Fitzgerald, Emily. "Towards a Famine Art History: Invention, Reception, and Repetition from the Nineteenth Century to the Twentieth." *Ireland's Great Hunger: Relief, Representation, and Remembrance.* Ed. David A. Valone. Lanham, MD: University Press, of America, 2010. 181–202. Print.

McLean, Stuart. *The Event and its Terrors: Ireland, Famine, Modernity.* Stanford, CA: Stanford University Press, 2004. Print.

Metscher, Priscilla. *James Connolly and the Reconquest of Ireland.* Minneapolis: MEP Publications, 2002. Print.

Moran, Gerard. *Sending out Ireland's Poor: Assisted Emigration to North America in the Nineteenth Century.* Dublin: Four Courts, 2004. Print.

Morash, Chris, ed. *The Hungry Voice: The Poetry of the Irish Famine*. Dublin: Irish Academic Press, 1989. Print.

---."Literature, Memory, Atrocity." *Fearful Realities: New Perspectives on the Famine*. Eds. Chris Morash and Richard Hayes. Dublin: Irish Academic Press, 1996. 110–18. Print.

---. *Writing the Irish Famine*. Oxford: Oxford University Press, 1995. Print.

Nally, David. P. *Human Encumbrances: Political Violence and the Great Irish Famine*. Notre Dame, IN: University of Notre Dame Press, 2011. Print.

Nassau Senior, W. *Journals, Conversations and Essays Relating to Ireland*. Vol. 1. London: Longmans and Greene, 1868.

Ó Gráda, Cormac. *Ireland's Great Famine: Interdisciplinary Perspectives*. Dublin: UCD Press, 2006. Print.

O'Malley, Ernie. "The Paintings of Jack B. Yeats." 1945. *Jack B. Yeats: A Centenary Gathering*. Ed. Roger McHugh. Dublin: Dolmen Press, 1971. Print.

O'Rourke, (Canon) John. *History of the Great Irish Famine*. Dublin: McGlashan and Gill, 1875. Print.

Orwell, George. "Notes on Nationalism." *Polemic*, no. 1 October 1945, reprinted in *The Collected Essays. Vol. 3, 1943–1945*. Harmondsworth: Penguin, 1974. Print.

Osborne, Rev. S. Godolphin. *Gleanings in the West of Ireland*. London: T. and W. Boone, 1850. Print.

O'Sullivan, Niamh. *Aloysius O'Kelly: Art, Nation, Empire*. Dublin: Field Day, 2010. Print.

---. "Lines of Sorrow: Representing Ireland's Great Hunger." *Ireland's Great Hunger Museum Inaugural Catalogue*. Hamden, CT: Quinnipiac University, 2012. Print.

Póirtéir, Cathal. "Folk Memory and the Famine." *The Great Irish Famine*. Ed. Cathal Póirtéir. Cork: Mercier Press, 1995. 219–31. Print.

Rigney, Ann. *Imperfect Histories: The Elusive Past and the Legacy of Romantic Historicism*. Ithaca: Cornell University Press, 2001. Print.

Rockett, Kevin and Emer Rockett. *Magic Lantern, Panorama and Moving Slide Shows in Ireland, 1786–1909*. Dublin: Four Courts Press, 2011. Print.

Sennett, Richard. *The Fall of Public Man*. 1974. London: Faber and Faber, 1986. Print.

Sexton, Sean. *Ireland: Photographs 1840–1930*. Introduction by J. J. Lee. London: Lawrence King, 1994. Print.

Sexton, Sean, and Christine Kinealy. *The Irish: A Photohistory, 1840–1940*. London: Thames and Hudson, 2002. Print.

Somerville, Alexander. *Letters from Ireland During the Famine of 1847*. Ed. K. M. D. Snell. Dublin: Irish Academic Press, 1994. Print.

"Sketches in the West of Ireland." *The Illustrated London News*, February 13, 1847.

Sontag, Susan. *On Photography*. 1977. London: Penguin, 1979. Print.

Swift, Jonathan. "Thoughts on Various Subjects." *Prose Writings of Jonathan Swift*. IV. Ed. Herbert Davis. Oxford: Oxford University Press, 1957. Print.

Taylor, A. J. P. *From Napoleon to the Second International: Essays on Nineteenth-Century Europe*. 1947. London: Hamish Hamilton, 1993. Print.

Trollope, Anthony. *Castle Richmond*. 1860. London: Penguin, 1993. Print.

Williams, Richard D'Alton. "Lord of Hosts." 1848. *The Hungry Voice: The Poetry of the Irish Famine*. Ed. Chris Morash. Dublin: Irish Academic Press, 1989. Print.

Woodham-Smith, Cecil. *The Great Hunger: Ireland 1845–1849*. 1962. London: Penguin, 1991. Print.

Yeats, W. B. "Introduction." *Oxford Book of Modern Verse*. Oxford: Oxford University Press, 1936. Print.

IMAGES

Cover / Figure 1
Micheal Farrell
1940–2000

Black '47
1997–98
Hillier's medium and acrylic on canvas
118 x 177 in
© Estate of Micheal Farrell

Figure 2
Photo of *Black '47* in Ireland's Great Hunger Museum

Figure 3
Pádraic Reaney
b. 1952

Departure [detail]
Oil on masonite
30 x 21 in
© 1996 Pádraic Reaney

Figure 4
Rowan Gillespie
b. 1953

Statistic I and *Statistic II*
2010
Bronze
Statistic I: 49 x 19 x 19 in
Statistic II: 49 x 19 x 13 in
© 1996–1998 Rowan Gillespie

Figure 5
Willoughby Wallace Hooper
1837–1912

Madras Famine Victims
1878
Photograph
The John Hillelson Collection, London
Image provided by Royal Geographical Society

Figure 6
James Mahony

"Village of Moveen"
The Illustrated London News
December 22, 1849

Figure 7
James Mahony

"Boy and Girl at Cahera"
The Illustrated London News
February 20, 1847

Figure 8
"Bridget O'Donnel and Children"
The Illustrated London News
December 22, 1849

Figure 9
Lilian Lucy Davidson
1879–1954

Gorta
1946
Oil on canvas
17.5 x 35.5 in
© Estate of Lilian Lucy Davidson

Figure 10
Alanna O'Kelly
1966

No Colouring Can Deepen the Darkness of Truth
1994–2012
Compilation of still images from video installation
© 1992 Alanna O'Kelly

Figure 11
Robert George Kelly

An Ejectment in Ireland (A Tear and a Prayer for Erin)
1848-1851
Owned by Anthony John Mourek
Image provided by Irish Arts Review

Figure 12
Queen Victoria Letter [detail]
1847

Figure 13
Geraldine O'Reilly
1956

The Deserted Village
2012
Photo etchings
1 of 8 panels, 14 x 16.5 in
© 2012 Geraldine O'Reilly

Figure 14
Dorothy Cross

Endarken
From "LANDscape" part of The Golden Bough Exhibition, 2008, Dublin City Gallery The Hugh Lane
Image courtesy of the artist and Kerlin Gallery, Dublin

Figure 15
Brian Maguire
b. 1951

The World is Full of Murder
1985
Acrylic on canvas
53 x 86 in
© 1985 Brian Maguire

Figure 16
"The Famine Queen"
L'Irlande Libre
April 1900
Image provided by Bibliothèque nationale de France

Figure 17
"Ireland Wrestles with Famine while Mr. Balfour Plays Golf"
United Ireland
August 23, 1890
Image provided by The National Library of Ireland

Figure 18
Margaret Allen
1830–1914

Bad News in Troubled Times
"An important arrest has been made, that of a young man named…"
The Freeman's Journal
1886
Oil on canvas
38 x 32 in

Images provided by Ireland's Great Hunger Museum, Quinnipiac University, unless noted otherwise.

ABOUT THE AUTHOR

Luke Gibbons is Professor of Irish Literary and Cultural Studies at
the National University of Ireland, Maynooth. He formerly taught at
the University of Notre Dame, U.S.A., and Dublin City University. His
publications include *Gaelic Gothic: Race, Colonialism and Irish Culture* (2004),
Edmund Burke and Ireland: Aesthetics, Politics and the Colonial Sublime (2003),
The Quiet Man (2002), *Transformations in Irish Culture* (1996), and co-wrote
(with Kevin Rockett and John Hill) *Cinema and Ireland* (1988). His book,
Joyce's Ghosts: Ireland, Modernism and Memory, is due for publication in 2015.

Quinnipiac University would like to thank the copyright holders
for granting permission to reproduce works illustrated in this book.
Every effort has been made to contact the holders of copyrighted
material. Omissions will be corrected in future editions if the
publisher is notified in writing.

All rights reserved. No part of this publication may be reproduced
or transmitted by any means, electronic or mechanical, including
photocopy, recording or any other storage and retrieval system,
without prior permission in writing from the publisher.

IRELAND'S GREAT HUNGER MUSEUM | QUINNIPIAC UNIVERSITY PRESS ©2014

SERIES EDITORS

Niamh O'Sullivan
Grace Brady

IMAGE RESEARCH

Claire Tynan

DESIGN / PRODUCTION MANAGEMENT

Group C Inc, New Haven
Brad Collins
Jessica Cassettari

ACKNOWLEDGMENT

Office of Public Affairs, Quinnipiac University

PUBLISHER

Quinnipiac University Press

PRINTING

GHP Media

ISBN 978-0-9904686-2-2

Ireland's Great Hunger Museum
Quinnipiac University

3011 Whitney Avenue
Hamden, CT 06518-1908
203-582-6500

www.ighm.org